MW01613517

Sisters in the Fruit Bowl

By

Sisters of the Tree

BLACK FOREST PRESS
The Tennessee Publishing House
496 Mountain View Drive
Mosheim, Tennessee 37818
423-422-4711

Sisters of the Tree

Pictured on the front cover, from left to right, are Sisters of the Tree authors: Mary Wagner, Paula Conner, Terrie Bryan, Patricia Cox, Joyce Thomasson, Jennie Sweeney and Ann Jamerson.

The authors are available for most any Christian speaking engagement or presentation dealing with the material in this book. They can be contacted at the Tree of Life Ministries. Call: (434) 851-1330

Sisters in the Fruit Bowl

By

Sisters of the Tree

Cover Designer: Joe Bivens
Cover Set-up:
Kellie Warren-Underwood

Disclaimer

This document is an original work of the author. It may include reference to information commonly known or freely available to the general public. Any resemblance to her published information is purely coincidental. The author has in no way attempted to use material not of her own origination. Black Forest Press disclaims any association with or responsibility for the ideas, opinions or facts as expressed by the author of this book. No dialogue is totally accurate or precise.

Scripture is taken from the King James Version (KJV) of the Holy Bible unless otherwise noted, as in NASB.

Printed in the United States of America
Library of Congress
Catalogue-in-Publication

ISBN: 978-1-59275-206-8
Copyright© 2008

ALL RIGHTS RESERVED

Experiencing the Fruit of the Spirit
Galations 5:22

FOREWORD

In our kitchen, we have a fruit bowl filled with fruit. One day our grandson, Braden, was over. He said he was hungry and went to the fruit bowl to pick up a piece of fruit. He then looked at me and asked, "Can I eat it?" I replied to his surprise by saying, "No, you cannot." He asked, "Why not?"

Little did he know or understand that the fruit in the fruit bowl was artificial. When I tried to explain about the fruit, I had to say things like, "It has no taste; it is only make believe; it only looks like the real thing; and it is hollow inside." He finally put down the fruit and walked away sad and disappointed.

Sisters in the Fruit Bowl has nothing artificial about it. This book speaks about real lives that were at one time hollow and tasteless—lives that looked good on the outside but were only skin deep.

With *Sisters in the Fruit Bowl,* you will not walk away disappointed but encouraged of how God can take the hollow and fill it with the fruit of the Spirit.

Pastor Mike Dodson
Tree of Life Ministries
Lynchburg, Virginia
www.tolm.net

ACKNOWLEDGEMENTS

To our Lord and Savior, Jesus Christ, who loved us enough to take our broken lives and put them back together with your mercy and grace.

To our families and friends, we are blessed to have you in our lives. Thank you for your love, prayers and encouragement.

Pastor Mike, we are honored to be a part of the vision that God has placed upon your life. Thank you for your prayers, support, and faith that you had in the "Sisters".

Roz Bush, We just can't thank you enough for the countless hours that you spent in editing our book. Thank you for your patience, words of wisdom, and your prayers. We love and appreciate you for using the gifts that God has blessed you with.

Joe Bivens, thank you for your ideas and many hours spent on designing our book cover.

Mark Conner, you have been such a blessing in answering numerous computer questions and for your wisdom in offering ideas while working on this project.

Tree of Life Staff and church family, we love and appreciate you for all of the support and encouraging words that were given throughout this process. We have definitely felt the Lord working through your prayers.

DEDICATION

To my Lord and Savior, Jesus Christ, who breathed
the words through me. To my mother and father,
Crawford and Mae Worley, my children, Christy,
Beth and Cheri. To my grandchildren Whitney,
Kayla, Luke, Stewart, Reagan and Cole.
                                              PATRICIA

To my Heavenly Father the Lover of my Soul. To
my parents, John and Gladys Perkins, and to Harold,
who are forever with our Lord. To my sister Rachel
who has always been there for me. To my children,
April, Dana and Wyatt, thank you for your love and
encouragement.
                                              JOYCE

To all my family, church family, and friends who
played a part in building my faith. You know who
you are.
                                              ANN

It is with love and much gratitude that I dedicate this
work. First to a Loving God who has, through His
grace and healing power, transformed and restored
my broken life. He has given me beauty for ashes.
Then to my family, who labored with me both
through the restoration of my life and ultimately
through this publication.
                                              TERRI

To my Lord and Savior, Jesus Christ. Without Him
I would be absolutely nothing. He is my Healer, my
Restorer, my Husband and all that I will ever need.
He alone gets all the glory for anything that I am or
ever will be.

JENNIE

I dedicate this to my loving husband, Mark for
always encouraging me to go after God with my
whole heart, and for being there for me as I have
gone through my growing pains. Through your walk
with the Lord you always inspire *me* to walk closer
to the Lord. I thank you for your servant's heart!

PAULA

I would like to dedicate my participation in this
book to my parents, Richard and Ruby Coffey, who
lived to see me enjoying my life. To my husband,
Dave, who always lets me follow God, wherever He
may lead. To my children, Jimmy and Lynda, my
grandchildren, Chris and Kaylea—may they experience even greater Joy as they seek God for their own
lives.

MARY

TABLE OF CONTENTS

INTRODUCTION

This book will perhaps enlarge your understanding and explain what the Fruit of the Spirit looks like in our everyday lives. To have the Fruit of the Spirit means we can function in an ungodly world, using our Godly gifts.

We are never far away from our Creator or His awesome plan for our lives. He can take our worst days and turn them into something useful.

We are not here to live a "charmed" life. We are here to let God "show-up" and "show-off" in our lives—to take what looks all wrong and make it right.

When the disasters of this world are piling up all around you, there is one who will see you through.

All of these attributes, Love, Peace, Joy, Goodness, Gentleness, Kindness, Long Suffering, Faithfulness and Self Control are not only *from* Him, they are *of* Him. His character and His feelings for you are all of these:

He is the God of *LOVE*. He loves you with an everlasting love.

He is the God of *PEACE*. He wants you to be whole, nothing missing, nothing broken.

He is the God of *JOY*. He lives inside of you that you may enjoy your life.

He is the God of *FAITHFULNESS*. He has faith in you, even when you don't.

He is the God of *LONGSUFFERING*. He has seen you through long years of denial, disobedience, and fear—just to bring you out into a spacious place.

He is the God of *GOODNESS, KINDNESS AND GENTLENESS*.

xii   Sisters of the Tree

With these attributes He can woo you to Himself and change you to be more like Jesus.

He is the God of *SELF CONTROL*. This attribute is a little different from the others. To have self control we have to participate with a desire to be controlled by God. God will give you, by His Love, a desire to obey Him and with that desire the power to please Him.

The Fruit of the Spirit is the outward evidence to the world that we have chosen Jesus Christ to be our example, our "live-in" teacher. And we have not only invited Him in, but we are fascinated by His instruction and eager to please Him.

As you read, examine your life; look at yourself up close. Is the evidence of God's Supernatural Spirit working in your life? Let the Word of God and the love of God awaken a new focus in your life—summiting to the Spirit.

Patricia Corpier
Isaiah 52:6

PEACE

*"How beautiful upon the mountains
are the feet of Him who brings good
news, who proclaims peace."*

Isaiah 52:7

Life is full of journeys. They take us down many paths in all kinds of directions. Sometimes they take us down paths of happiness and joy beyond anything we could ever imagine. Other times the paths lead us to loneliness, pain, despair and grief. It was down the path of loneliness and despair that I learned the true meaning of what Jesus meant when He said, *"....I will never leave you nor forsake you"* (Heb. 13:5).

On September 11, 2005, my life changed suddenly. My beloved mother lost her battle with cancer. She learned she had brain cancer in June of that year. And just two and a half months later, she went home to be with Jesus.

My mother and I were very close. We talked on the phone almost every day. I called her early in the morning before my day got busy, and I visited her at least once a week. We went on walks in the park and took little shopping trips. We visited relatives we hadn't seen for a while. Occasionally, we went to see some of her favorite bands. Mom especially liked Blue Grass gospel music. But whatever we did together made her happy.

My mother loved Christmas; it was her favorite time of year. This day brought all of her family together. Her children, grandchildren and great grandchildren, who were gathered around her, gave her more joy than any other gift we could have given.

Mom was always loving and caring. I remember the first time she came home from the hospital after being diagnosed with terminal cancer. I sat on her lap hugging her tight. I asked her forgiveness for anything I had ever said or done to hurt her. She hugged me back just as tight and said, "Patricia, you have never done anything wrong to me." My heart ached because I knew that I had. But my mother saw nothing bad because she had already forgiven me before I asked.

My mother never complained about her illness. She did say, "I wish I wasn't sick." Moreover, she questioned herself, wondering if she had done something wrong that caused her illness. Her pastor came to her home, talked with her, and offered the peace she needed. Mother loved the Lord and knew exactly where she would be spending eternity. Yet the morning she slipped away from us came all too soon.

Losing my mother left my world filled with pain and sorrow. I knew she was in Heaven, but the grief I felt was unbearable. I was filled with guilt and shame, knowing I should have done so much more for her than I had. My heart was broken, and I felt so all alone. My days were filled with tears and loneliness. The valley I was in seemed dark and without end—deep with no way out.

It has been almost two years now since I lost my mother. I still miss her and think about her every day. But I want to say here, the valley I was in did have a way out. I was never in there alone. Jesus was with me through the pain, the loneliness and the darkness. He held me in His loving arms while I wept my tears of grief. He gave me peace and comfort that no one else could give in my time of suffering (John 14:7).

The journey through this valley seemed so long but with each new day, Jesus brought me closer to the end of the long road I had to travel. Then came the day He carried me out of that valley onto the mountain top. Oh, what a beautiful place to be, on the mountaintop. Joy, peace and restoration were waiting for me there.
I know there will be other valleys to go through, but I will not have to go alone. He will always be with me.

I'm on another journey now. I call it my journey for Jesus—a journey that will take me down a path with Jesus leading where He wants me to go. I'm praying every step of the way to do His will, not mine. He has a plan for my life and a vision. And He is going to breathe life into them when it's time. This journey hasn't been easy either. Satan always stands ready to steal what God has for me. But I have come to trust in the promise of God's Word: *"The Lord is not slack concerning His promises..."* (2 Peter 3:9). I walk arm in arm with my Savior; we talk, we laugh, and I cry tears of joy, tears of love, and sadness. I sing praises to Him even when I can't seem to feel His presence.

I know He's still with me. Praising Him brings my Lord close, and I can hear Him whisper, "Come take my hand, so that I can give you comfort and rest from your weariness." I go to Him and take His nail-pierced hand and feel the sweet gentleness of peace flowing through me. I lie at His feet and worship Him, for there is no place I'd rather be than at the feet of Jesus, my King, my Savior, my everything. He will be your everything too, if you'll let Him. Jesus has given us a free choice.

"In the last day, that great day of the feast, Jesus stood and cried saying, *"...If any one thirst, let him come to me and drink."* (John 7:37). He is the living water and the bread of life. When you eat and drink of Jesus, you will never be hungry or thirsty again. There is nothing in this world that can fill you and satisfy the way that Jesus can. Who or what will you choose—the world that offers nothing but false hope or a loving Savior?

He came to earth from heaven to suffer and die on a cross so that you and I can have eternal life. He loves us that much. Death couldn't hold Him. I serve a risen Savior. What about you? It's your choice. He's waiting. He will wash away your sin. He will heal your broken heart. You have grown so tired and weary. Darkness and despair are all around you. "Come." He whispers to you. "Come and give it all to me. I will give you rest."

Can you hear His gentle voice calling?

I think I'll go now and sit at the feet of my King for awhile and just praise Him for all He has done for me. I'll praise Him for all He has brought me through; I'll thank Him for giving me a new heart. Want you come and go with me?

"Now the fruit of righteousness is sown in peace by those who make peace" (James 3:18).

"Peace I leave with you; my peace I give to you, not as this world gives do I give to you" (John 14:27).

"Let the peace of Christ rule in your hearts since as members of one body you were called to peace and be thankful" (Col. 3:15).
"And the peace of God which surpasses all understanding will guard your hearts and minds through Christ Jesus" (Phil. 4:7).

Prayer:

Heavenly Father,
I thank you for the peace that lives in my heart—peace that only you can give. Thank you for your love, mercy and forgiveness. Most of all, thank you for your Son Jesus, the Prince of Peace.

Patricia Cox

Joyce Thomasson
Matt 22:37

LOVE

"But now faith, hope, love, abide, these three;
But the greatest of these is love."

1 Corinthians 13:13

"Jesus loves me; this I know." At least that's what people at church told me. As a young child growing up in the 50's, I saw pictures of a smiling Jesus with children gathered around him, happy families going to church together, and children having fun. But as I looked at my life, it didn't quite look like the pictures I saw in Sunday school.

I remember one day in particular when I was three years old. I stood and watched my mother twist her short dark hair up close to her head with her finger and slide a bobby pin over the curl to secure it. I loved to sit at the old vanity and pretend I was my mother. Sometimes, she let me put a little of her bright red lipstick on. Then she patted my lips with a tissue leaving red lip prints on it.

This day was different. It would leave memories in my mind for years to come. I can still see my father walking quickly out the door around the side of our small white frame house. He jumped into his parked car in the backyard and left.

Feeling something was wrong, I ran after him as fast as my three-year-old legs could run. My mother followed close behind. She swept me off my feet and held me close. She said, "You can't go with Daddy this time."

Months later, my daddy came back and brought me a small windmill to put in the yard. When the wind blew, the wooden man sawed back and forth on a log. I loved that little windmill, and I loved my daddy for coming back home to see me.

My mother told me, out of her pain, that my dad had left us. Worse than that, she said he didn't love us anymore. I heard that cruel statement for what seemed like forever. But later I found out differently. My daddy did love me.

Over the next few years, I saw him a lot more. My mother didn't have a driver's license when I was growing up, so my father and his new family would pick us up and take us to visit my grandparents who lived about an hour away. Traveling back home one day from visiting some of the family in Halifax, an argument broke out in the car. Although I was only five, I remember as if it were yesterday. I listened until I couldn't listen any longer. All of a sudden, I screamed out, "I wish I was dead!" Silence fell. My family must have been shocked to hear that statement coming from a five-year-old.

How that day ended I don't remember. As far as that goes, I can't even recall the next year. But, when I started attending elementary school, the kids would whisper when they saw me and make hurtful comments to me about my family. I felt so ashamed.

As I grew, I realized that my mom *and* dad loved me. Even though they didn't live together, they were always there for me. My mother worked hard ironing clothes and cleaning houses for people from our church and other neighbors. That way, she could keep things going at home and put me through school.

I didn't have a lot of things growing up, but one thing I did have was a loving mother. She kept me by her side and taught me the importance of going to church and loving God. She taught me to love other people, even if they had hurt me.

One Christmas, it snowed so deep we couldn't get out of the house. There was no way I would have a present under the tree. I walked into the living room of our three-room house that Christmas morning and looked under the tall cedar tree. Underneath was a small package with my name on it. When I opened the present, my mother's only watch was positioned neatly in the box. I realized that she had given up her watch so that I could have a gift. At that moment I knew I had the best mom in the world. She loved me and wanted to give me the desires of my heart. That wasn't the only sacrifice she made for me growing up. For many years she prayed and worked at making my life easier than hers had been.

We attended church every time the door was opened—rain or shine. That was a major part of my life. At a Friday night revival, I heard a man preach on hell. He told how Jesus died on a cross to give us life everlasting. Then I realized that Jesus did love me, no matter what I had gone through as a little girl. He wanted me to be in Heaven with Him one day. So that night, at age nine, I asked God to forgive me of my sins—especially for the time I wished I was dead. I really wanted to live.

I looked out in the sanctuary at my best friend, thinking, "Why aren't you coming up to the altar? Don't you feel God touching your heart like I do?" I didn't understand why she wasn't asking Jesus to come into her heart. Surely she didn't want to go to hell like the preacher said. The Bible says, "...now is the day of salvation" (2 Corinthians 6:2). Yet we can't force anyone to accept Him. It's their choice.

As I grew, not only physically but spiritually, I read and experienced the love of God in my life, as well as my family's love for me. The white wooden swing hanging on our front porch became my special place to read God's Word. I not only read but memorized chapters that I later quoted in front of a large congregation of area churches. One time, girls from several churches had studied scripture over the year. Then at a special service, they would be awarded for their work in missions. My part was to quote 1Corinthians 13:1-13, the love chapter of the Bible.

These scriptures have been very dear to my heart all my life. Many times I wondered if God wanted these verses to be planted deep within me as a reminder that He loves me and He wants me to know how to love others.

I loved this time in my life, but as I approached my teenage years, I didn't put God first anymore. Instead, I moved Him down the list a little bit. God's Word says He's our first love (Revelation 2:4). However, I found another love that I quickly put into first place. For the next three years of my life, my boyfriend—who later became my husband—was first. My time with God became extremely limited.

Soon after my sixteenth birthday, I not only had a husband but a few months down the road, I had a baby girl who needed a lot of my time. Sure, I continued to go to church and even taught youth and children, sang in the choir, got involved in a young woman's mission group, and helped with some cottage prayer meetings.

Yes, I had a family, a job, and *religion.* I allowed my personal time with God to become a distant third, fourth or fifth. Things were mostly about me and what I thought I needed to do to be a good Christian.

As a small child, I had felt unloved when my dad left. Later I found the Lord, fell in love with Him and enjoyed spending time with Him. But over the years, I traded my precious time with my Lord for doing good works. Although I had become what I thought was a good mother, wife, and worker in the church and on my job, I had lost the intimacy with my first love, Jesus.

When we walk away from our first love, we open the door for Satan to slip into our lives. And he did. Over a couple of years, I made many mistakes and took some wrong turns. All the while God was tugging at my heart to repent of the mess I was making out of my life.

My pastor asked if he could talk and pray with our family. But I said, "No, everything will be fine." I was stubborn, but God used that one simple request to turn my life around. Someone did notice my need for repentance and tried to reach out to me. Thank God, He looked beyond my faults and saw my need for Him. Joel 2:1

says, *"Return to the Lord your God, for He is gracious and compassionate, slow to anger and abounding in love."*

Praise God when we call upon His name, He is there to lift us up out of the miry clay and set our feet on the solid rock. That's exactly what He did for me. So I made a promise to God, "If You will get me out of this mess, I won't fall into this sin trap again." Sound familiar?

The next six months of my life were almost perfect. God had restored my marriage and family. My husband Harold and I had two beautiful girls and were teaching a young children's Sunday school class together. Life was just great!

Then came my 29th birthday, That evening I had to play softball for the church team. My husband Harold asked, "Would you mind if I go fishing while you're at the game?" Of course, he always supported me in what I did, so I told him, "That's fine with me."

At around nine-thirty that night, I arrived back home, but Harold wasn't there yet. So I started cleaning. Then I cut the grass in the dark with the porch light on. After that, the girls and I went to bed. At four o'clock in the morning, I woke up startled by the door bell ringing. Somehow, I made it to the door and looked out. There stood my pastor and a policeman on the porch.

I opened the door, already knowing in my spirit that my husband was dead. Why else would they be here in the middle of the night? My husband had run into the side of an underpass about two miles from our home. He had been partially thrown from his pickup truck. Harold's life ended that night. But even though I was standing there, I felt like my life had ended too.

Over the next weeks and months, my two-year-old daughter Dana constantly asked, "When is Daddy coming home?" My twelve-year-old April had been very close to her dad. Yet, she never said a word about him for the next year. I felt as if every ounce of life had been drained from me. I didn't know what to do or say to anyone. I dreaded going back to work to face people, and the last thing I wanted to hear was another, "I'm sorry to hear about your husband." Loneliness overwhelmed me. The thought of my girls not having a father at home reminded me of my own childhood.

Thank God for Faye, my Sunday school teacher. She loved me enough to give me some wise counsel. Faye said, "Take the time you spent with your husband and spend that same time with the Lord."

My first thought was that was going to be hard, since I had spent a lot of time with my husband. But I figured it sure wouldn't hurt to try. So, over the next few months, I put Him first in my life and built a relationship again with my first love. People sometimes asked me about raising my daughters alone. But I told them, "I'm raising them with their heavenly Father's help."

Over the following years, I started making wrong choices again, not fully allowing God's will to be done in all things. Eventually, I was doing what I promised God that I wouldn't do again. When I stepped out in my will instead of God's, I suffered the consequences.

I fell back into the old routine of putting works before intimacy with my Lord. Therefore, I missed out on God's full blessing for my life. I thought I knew what loving God was all about. Instead, I found myself looking for approval and love from people, not God. I developed a critical spirit towards people who weren't living the way I thought they should. Instead of helping or praying for them, my solution was to talk about them. I had forgotten what my dad told me growing up, "If you can't say something nice about someone, don't say anything at all!"

Over the next eight years, I was a single mom raising my two girls. I spent time with my family and friends and was faithful to my church. Then in the fall of 1991, I met a young man—John. We fell in love, and six months later we were married. Two years later, God blessed us with a baby boy—John Wyatt. He had blonde hair, blue eyes, and was cuter than I could have ever imagined. Shortly after Wyatt's birth, John met a man named Dennis. He was a preacher, a man God placed into our lives. He invited us to attend his home church with him. The problem for me was that I had been a Baptist girl for forty years, and this church wasn't quite my style. It was Pentecostal!

In my old church, I was used to sitting up front and being a part of everything going on. But in the Pentecostal church I found myself praying that no one would be sitting on the back row where I wanted to be. I didn't understand hands going up in the air and people saying, "Amen!" and shouting. My thought was, "Oh Lord, help me!" But, to please my new husband, I continued going with him. The people were very friendly and showed us love at every service. So after *much* prayer, I joined the church along with my husband.
I realized that for years, I had been living in my will instead of God's. And I became very dissatisfied with my attitude. Because I wanted to work on my spiritual walk with God, I began watching some senior ladies at our new little church. I saw something in them that I didn't have, and I wanted to know more about that. They had a genuine love for God and other people. You could see the love of God in their eyes. And when they prayed for you, it felt as if God himself was standing there with you, reaching into the depths of your heart. They lifted their hands in praise and thanksgiving as tears flowed down their cheeks. Yes, I wanted that kind of relationship with my God. I was tired of religion and works. I wanted to know Jesus like they did.

I began praying earnestly for God to let me love people with His heart, to see them through His eyes, to serve them with His hands and to follow in His footsteps. This prayer went on for weeks. One Tuesday morning at a prayer service, I said the prayer again. When my eyes opened, I felt like the blind man that Jesus healed. Everyone in the prayer circle looked different; even the paint on the walls seemed brighter. I wanted to hug everyone and say, "I love you." I was a new woman in Christ. He had answered my prayers. Now I had the ability to love people and see them in a different light.

Since that awesome day of spiritual healing, I have been in hot pursuit of my Savior, my Father, the Lover of my soul. I hunger and thirst after Him, to be intimate with Him, and to allow Him to use me to show His love to others.

Although I still make my share of mistakes, my heavenly Father is quick to open my eyes to them. Then He shows me mercy and grace.

When you put all your energy into doing good works, pleasing others rather than God, and looking for happiness and love from other people, you'll find yourself disappointed and miserable.

I encourage you to hunger and thirst after righteousness. Let God have control of your life and all its circumstances. He said, "...I will never leave you nor forsake you," (Deuteronomy 31:6). He's waiting for you to let Him into your heart, to love you, to save you and to give you life, and life more abundantly.

Now I don't want to live one single moment without Him. Thank God, when we are saved, He places inside of us the fruit of the Spirit—love, joy, peace, faith, meekness, gentleness, goodness, self-control and patience. We as Christians have all of these, but we must allow the Holy Spirit to work them out through us. It doesn't come overnight; it's a lifelong process. Because we want to be like Jesus, we try to live a righteous and holy life. He wants us to love Him, love others, and to love ourselves.

Seeking to be all we can be for Christ, seeking not only His hands but His face, I long for Him. I want to love him, to serve Him, and to praise Him. He is worthy.

Now when I think about I Corinthians 13:1-13, it's not just a passage that I memorized as a child. These are words that I want to live by every day.

It's the Excellence of Love.

"Love is patient, love is kind, and is not jealous; love does not brag and is not arrogant, does not act unbecomingly; it does not seek its own, is not provoked, does not take into account a wrong suffered, does not rejoice in unrighteousness, but rejoices with the truth; bears all things, believes all things, hopes all things, endures all things. Love never fails" (1 Corinthians 13:4-8). NASB

Prayer:

Dear Heavenly Father,
I want to thank you for loving me enough to die for my sins. Lord, please help me to see others through your eyes, to love them with your heart, and to serve them with your hands. Help me to follow in your footsteps and to live by your example that you set for me. In Jesus name I pray. Amen

Joyce Thomasson

Ann Janesh II Cor 12:9

FAITH

"...The just shall live by faith" Romans 1:17.

Are you suffering crop failure? Is the fruit of your life dying on the vine? Are you in the middle of a drought? Walk by faith and not by sight if you want to see your crop improve. Develop a vital union with Christ. The fruit of love, joy, peace and faith deals with the inner self. If we possess the fruit of the Spirit, we can also walk in the Spirit. (Gal. 5:25). How then should I live? The apostle Paul tells us, *"...The just shall live by faith"* (Romans 1:17).

What is faith? It is totally depending on God. Faith is fidelity which makes one true to his promises and faithful to his task. *"Now faith is the substance of things hoped for and the evidence of things not seen"* (Heb 11:1). We walk by faith, not by sight, so walk every day with eternity's values in view.

How do we get faith? It is part of the fruit of the Spirit. *"So then faith comes by hearing, hearing by the word of God"* (Romans 10:17). Being born again gives us faith.

One day I came face to face with this question, "What will you do with this man called Jesus?" He wants to be your Savior and Lord. God loves you so much. *"For God so loved the world that He gave His only begotten Son that whosoever believes in him will not perish but have everlasting life"* (John 3:16).

I was 21 when I read in the Bible that I was a sinner because of the sin of Adam, the first man. *"Therefore ,just as through one man (Adam), sin entered the world and death through sin and thus death spread to all men, because all sinned"* (Romans 5:12). I knew I was a sinner and needed a Savior. I heard God's word. I believed it and was born again. *"That if you confess with your mouth the Lord Jesus and believe in your heart that God has raised Him from the dead, you will be saved."* (Romans 10:9).

Experiencing being born again began my walk of faith. As my faith began to grow, I experienced what I call building blocks of faith. These blocks are circumstances that come into our lives. Romans 8:28-29 states, *"And we know that all things work together for good to those who love God, to those who are the called according to his purpose. For whom he foreknew, he also predestined to be conformed to the image of his Son, that he might be the firstborn among many brethren."* I didn't know it at that time but there would be many times in my life when I would go back to these verses and say, "Yes God, I trust you. You are conforming me to the image of Christ."

Each of these experiences have been a part of my life and are faith-building. We make a choice each time blocks come in our life. Will I trust God? Can I look death in the eye and say, "Yes Lord, even in death I trust you. I will keep eternity's values in view."

September 3, 1980 I received a phone call from the Newark, NJ police department. "Your husband's hotel room was broken into; he's been shot; it is very serious. Come as soon as possible."

W. C. had left home the day before, going to pick up automobiles for our family business. I had heard someone say, "One phone call can change the whole course of your life." This is so true. Later that day when I arrived at the hospital, I was told my husband had died. My whole world turned inside out and upside down. When the dearest person in the world to us is gone, we cling to God's promises. He will never leave us or forsake us.

I faced many decisions. One hard question was, "How will I survive financially?" I was 39 with a ten-year-old child. My three sons were grown, ages 19 through their early twenties. At that time, God supernaturally provided for us with a settlement because the hotel lacked security. Later, through the help of a close friend, my sons started a business with automobiles. God has blessed that venture mightily.

Do I have much to praise God for? Yes. He has never left me, never forsaken me. He is my provider. I try to keep eternity's values in view. My separation from W.C. is temporary. I will see him in Heaven.

Sixteen years later on the anniversary of W.C.'s death, I once again faced a major question. "Will I trust God in the face of adversity?" My life was full. I was happy as I traveled and shared my story of salvation and life through Stonecroft Ministries. Yet, my vision seemed a little blurry. So I went to have my eyes examined, thinking I needed new glasses. The news I received was devastating, "You have an incurable eye condition." As I read the pamphlet the doctor gave me, I realized I could go blind. There is no cure for my condition. "Lord, how will I make it?"

Three friends called me that day sharing about Jesus in the Garden of Gethsemane. He prayed to God, His heavenly Father, "Not my will but thy will be done." This assured me, "Ann, this is what God wants you to know."

Three years later, I am legally blind, which means I can't drive a car. Yet, God has provided. Several times He has provided the very best doctors. Furthermore, He has sent someone to live in my home, so I have transportation. Another special friend drives me to speaking engagements. And my current treatment has held my vision at the same level for eight years! That is a miracle in itself. I still see well enough to read with a video eye.

Do I have much to thank God for? Yes, I do. He will make a way when there seems to be no way. I am reminded once again, *"For we walk by faith, not by sight"* (II Cor. 5:7). Romans 8:28 and 29 are once again on my mind as I experience this building block of faith.

Then came another faith builder. I was serving God and happy in my walk with Him. However, when I went to the doctor for a routine check-up, the doctor said, "You have cancer." Could I contin-

ue to trust God? The road ahead was uncharted territory. I wondered, "What will it be like? Will I live? What can I expect?" As
family and friends prayed, I was reassured of God's love and presence.
First came an operation. Then I was faced with chemotherapy and
radiation. I prayed about the doctors who were to give me this
treatment. God led me to Medical College of Virginia in
Richmond. Through it all, God was so good to me. I didn't experience the nausea and sickness that so many patients do. Was it
hard? Yes. Was God with me? Absolutely.

While at M.C.V. I had opportunities to share my faith with several
people. Once in a waiting room I engaged in conversation with a
young girl who was a driver for a cancer patient. She asked me
what I spoke about when I traveled. "I speak about how you can
know Jesus, and how we can know we are going to heaven." Then
she asked me, "Can you tell me how I can know?" I shared with
her. We had a room full of people. God had this plan as well as
many others while I was in Richmond, VA. I finished my treatment
in 2004.

As I write, it is 2008. During that time of illness, I came face to
face with the thought, "Will I live or will I die?" I realized I certainly was in a win-win situation. If I went to heaven I would see
Jesus. All sickness would be gone. If God chose to heal me, I
would stay and serve Him a little longer. He chose to heal me.
Now God is giving me some awesome assignments. He is my
Healer (Jeremiah 30:17a).

In recent days my faith has been increased as I watch my sister-in-
law Bertha and my nephews, Zeke and Michael Ben, the family of
my late brother Mike. I am reminded of the faithfulness of God and
His answer to the prayers of my brother.

My heart sank as I walked out the bedroom door. I had just told my
baby brother, "I'll see you again." I knew it would be in heaven.
The last six years had been a bittersweet experience as I watched

Mike battle cancer. But, I also saw him walk a victory walk with Jesus. There had been many spiritual conversations over the years. My mind went back to the day Mike came home as a new-born baby. I was a young teenager much in awe of the little boy. It was sort of a family joke because I have large feet; that day I looked at Mike and said, "Yes, he ours; he has big feet." I remember times I spent with Mike as a little boy, reading to him and answering numerous questions. He was always inquisitive and bright. I think of him as a happy child, a straight-A student, singing in the children's choir at church, and always like a shadow to our daddy.

In Mike's young teens our daddy went home to be with the Lord. All I can say is I saw Mike's world fall apart. I saw him looking for a place to belong. Sad to say, it took many years of floundering before he came face to face with the reality of needing to get his life straight. Many times I had talked with him about his life, but God had an appointed time when Mike would look to Him.

It was about seven years ago when I stood by Mike's bed at the hospital. His illness had just begun. I remember being there looking at a very disgruntled and unhappy young man. I thought, "What a waste of a life." Mike was in a stormy marriage. He had two beautiful boys, whom he loved with all his heart. I left the hospital that day praying for Mike. Hours later I received a phone call hours later saying Mike wanted me to return to the hospital. As I entered his room, Mike said, "I think I need to get my life right with God." This began a walk of about six years, of battling cancer and at the same time growing stronger in his quest toward God. The Tree of Life church family loved Mike and really reached out to him and his family. I took praise and worship tapes to Mike and he listened to them. He told me, "You know, it just lifts me up above all my problems." We had many conversations as I was also battling cancer. I remember we talked about how he might get to heaven first, but I would be there soon. He said, "Don't be sad when I'm gone; be happy." As I sat with him many times at church I watched Mike's faith growing. I also saw his burden for his family.

One Saturday, a friend and I went to Mike's home because he was very sick. That day we led Bertha to a saving knowledge of Jesus. Then we went in the bedroom to tell Mike how God had answered his prayer. To my surprise, Mike, Bertha, Zeke and Michael were at church the next morning. Mike Dodson, our pastor, asked the church to pray together for Mike's family. That afternoon God answered prayer again as Tommy Tucker, the youth pastor, led Zeke and Michael Ben to the Lord. I remember saying, "Well Mike, how is that for God answering your prayers?"

Two weeks later I asked Mike, "Can you trust God with your boys?" Mike's family was first and foremost on his mind. His answer to my question was, "Yes." Mike had told me he did not want to go until he knew they would be okay. So Mike went to heaven knowing God would take care of his family. Is my faith increased by this? Yes, it is. I am witnessing a miracle of God's grace as I see Bertha, Zeke and Michael Ben serving God.

I go to the Bible and read God's promises. He has never disappointed me. It's a walk of faith, not seeing, yet believing God's promises. Faith is depending on God, keeping eternity's values in view. One day we will be home in heaven with the family of God. All sickness, sorrow and pain will be gone. We'll spend eternity with Jesus, our Savior and Lord. We will hear God say how pleased He is that we trusted Him when we could not see.

Faith is built on trusting God's word and who He is. God is my El Roi, "the God who sees." He is Jehovah Jireh, "the Lord will provide." He is Jehovah Shalom, "the Lord is peace." He is Jehovah Shammah, "the Lord is there." Hallelujah! Yes, He is!

Prayer:

Dear God,
Help me to daily feed upon Your Word that my faith might grow.

Ann Jamerson

Phil 4:13
Jennie Bryan

LONG-SUFFERING

*"For I am convinced that neither death, nor life,
nor angels, nor principalities, nor things present,
nor things to come, nor powers, nor height, nor
depth, nor any other created thing, will be able to
separate us from the love of God, which is in
Christ Jesus our Lord."*

Romans 8:38-39

The journey through this life in Christ, our Redeemer and Lord, has its glorious mountain tops. However, it also has its deep, dark valleys. Yet I believe the Holy Spirit offers us His power to help us get through life. Yes, we must forge through, as David, the psalmist, said, "Yea *though I walk through the valley of the shadow of death, I will fear no evil, for Thou art with me... Thy rod and thy staff, they comfort me"* (Psalm 23:4*)*. However, one thing is required of us—prayer. Through prayer and much seeking I have experienced the gift of faith. That gift was everything to me when I had nothing else to cling to. When circumstances were lined up against me, He gave me peace beyond my comprehension. With this peace came unspeakable joy. Last, but most importantly, He has given me unconditional love.

My story is one of long-suffering. However, it is not unique. You may find that you can identify with my experiences, for they have been shared by countless others. I have found that Christ restores and heals through His power and the fruit of the Spirit. In Him, we have totally transformed lives. To God is the glory for His perfect redemption plan through His ultimate sacrifice. He was born to die, so that we may live, because of resurrection power. This was a fruit of the Spirit, long-suffering, love that suffered long, all for the joy that was set before Him.

"Consider Him who has endured such hostility by sinners against Himself, so that you will not grow weary and lose heart" (Hebrews 12:3).

Long-suffering is to surrender in obedience. Let me testify that our God loves us too much to leave us the way He found us. I'm never thrilled to speak of the past deeds of a sinful, yet broken, and spiritually dead woman. However, the Bible says, *"They overcame him because of the blood of the Lamb and because of the word of their testimony"* (Revelation 12:11).

When I was only three-years-old, evil made a bid for my soul. I was too young to even comprehend the gravity of incest. But my daddy, whom I trusted, crushed my spirit. With that unspeakable act, he ravaged my soul, leaving shame—too toxic to recover from. I was like a sheep being led to the slaughter. My self-worth was destroyed before it could even germinate. A flower that God intended to flourish had died. Those close to me could not see that I was only three, yet already dead. Innocence, that never trusted again, stayed stuck in a world of never-ending fear.

Satan waits anxiously for any of us who strays from the truth. When we are most vulnerable, *"...the devil, prowls around like a roaring lion, seeking someone to devour"* (1 Peter 5:8). My situation was tragic. But with time, God has used the evil, intended for my harm, for my good. Unfortunately, many years would pass before His purpose was revealed to me.

So this violent act, once perpetrated on me, began a perpetual cycle. As it continued, I became the walking dead, participating in what I had learned. *"Train up a child in the way he should go. Even when he is old he will not depart from it"* (Proverbs 22:6). However, the lesson I learned was: I am worthless. So I bought the lie. Now, to me, it was truth.

What a distortion for God's truth that we are *"fearfully and wonderfully made"* (Psalm 139:14). We were made in the image God, who is good. For God is love. I'm certain that many of you share my old belief system. For Satan does nothing new. He tells the same lies to infinite numbers of hurting people. The good news is that God, who also waits patiently, perseveres for His children. He does not want anyone to perish. Instead, he wants all of us to come to the saving knowledge of his son, Jesus.

This Loving Father continued to pursue me, even through the years of victimizing myself. I was promiscuous with men. Then there was anorexia, bulimia, some drugs, lots of alcohol, and many suicide attempts. There was still one part of me I needed to kill—the gnawing, ever constant raging ache. But instead of dying, it grew more intense with every lascivious act. God, however, was long-suffering. *"For we have not a high priest who can not sympathize with our weaknesses, but one who has been tempted in all things as we are, yet without sin"* (Hebrews 4:15). His was a love that suffered long for my repentance. Yet I suffered at my own hands, living in a constant state of sin.

God continued to woo me. As with Adam, in the garden, He called out, "Terrie, where are you?" I, like Adam, hid myself for I was ashamed. Continuing in my sin, I became pregnant. Once again, I was gripped with fear. I did what the world made easy and acceptable. I had an abortion. This time I had innocent blood on *my* hands. I used more alcohol to anesthetize my pain. Alcohol became my stronghold, the sin that took me down.

Broken, I finally came to the truth. I repented and received Jesus. However, I had little to no understanding and nothing that would sustain me. Yet my Savior still pursued me, with love that suffers long. By grace, and only grace, He pulled me away from my eating disorders, the drugs, the alcohol, and the promiscuous behaviors. I now realized I could not just stop these behaviors. I needed to heal from the reasons I did them. So I sought help through counseling. I was pursuing a healing that could only come from God. God had indeed saved me, at least from much sin. *"Where sin increased, grace abounded all the more"* (Romans 5:20).

Through the years of struggle and change, I met the man I would later marry. But even with all this, I didn't look to God as my source. I was still looking to man. My husband John and I stayed in a marriage with all the scars and unhealed wounds we both had brought with us. It definitely was not a marriage made in heaven. He was a man who loved me and our two beautiful children. However, he had broken places that made it impossible for him to love me with the deep intimacy that I needed.

He took care of us as a dependable father would. The roles between male and female, husband and wife were confused. I felt the care that a kind father would give, but I felt unloved as a woman. This confirmed to me again, that something must be wrong with me. Evil came back into my home in the form of pornography. Once again, I started drinking and going around a familiar mountain. In my unfulfilled state, I found myself vulnerable. Seduced back into sin, I committed adultery.

I left a marriage of fifteen years—from a man I knew loved me. I loved him too, but we were too broken to make it work. Neither of us understood unconditional love. We hadn't received it in our homes as children. I was violated by my father, and I suspect my husband's wounding went very deep as well. Two Christian people, with all our trying, couldn't save our dying marriage. He divorced me, and we shared custody of our children. It was devastating to all of us. I'd been wife and mother for so long; I soon realized that it was the only identity I ever had. My self-worth only came through others. Now without them, I felt worthless again. I was totally co-dependent.

At that point I was sharing an apartment with a co-worker from the restaurant where I waited tables. My roommate was a young gay man. Once again I went back into the bar scene. This time it was into the insidious world of the gay lifestyle. That included more drugs, and, of course, alcohol.

Removed from God, my life spiraled downward. I felt convicted as my life was now unmanageable. So I did what I knew to do, and I returned back to Alcoholics Anonymous—a program I had used throughout the years to stay sober. There I met my second husband Mark, thinking he also had a drinking problem. Only after we had married I discovered He had an addiction to crack cocaine.

My life became a nightmare. Of course, I ran back to God, went back into church, and virtually became a woman running from her drug-addicted husband. I couldn't see my son or daughter as often as I would have liked. Now the long-suffering was for their greater good. I needed to keep them out of harm's way when Mark was using drugs. That was more often than not.

Broken, I found myself crying out to God. He started to teach me about worship. What a healing He began, which continued to draw me closer. My walk with God started out as an act of desperation. Finally my Pastor Jerry made me realize that a drug-addicted and abusive husband was not part of God's will for any marriage. So we separated.

Then I had a good job selling furniture. I lived alone and saw my children as often as I could. The staying and leaving went on for a long time before the final act of legal separation from Mark. It had taken quite a toll on my children and me. All trust was gone—if there had ever been any—for any man. The abuse in so many ways was a flash from my past—the feelings of loss from my childhood. Now I had lost not one, but two, husbands. Now I was trying to live right, yet Satan was trying desperately to win control over me again. I was living one day at a time and did my best on my own as a working mother.

Life had been somewhat peaceful for a while, now that I was sober. With a legal separation and a restraining order in place, Mark, my drug-addicted husband, had finally left me alone. Then one day, out of the blue, my daughter called me to say, "Mom, you might want to know that Daddy has gone to the hospital."

He was in a great deal of pain. That night I was lying wide awake, wondering what was happening to my ex-husband John. In comparison to the sick man I was currently married to, John was not only a good father, but was still, in some ways, looking after me. Long-suffering was about to take on a whole new meaning.

When morning finally arrived, I made the call, praying it was nothing. It was cancer! Melanoma, which had metastasized to his liver, was in the fourth stage. A man I had never really let go of was about to die. My mind couldn't wrap itself around that. Now being faced with raising two fatherless children, I cried out to God once again, still not realizing that He never had left me. *"I will never desert you, nor will I ever forsake you"* (Hebrews 13:5).

Meanwhile my second husband had given his life to Christ. And because it seemed like the right thing to do, we reconciled. At that time—after the children's father died—I did not have the ability to make wise decisions. So there I was again, with a man who could not take care of himself, let alone a wife and two children.

Although the children's father had not been gone more than two months, I was still in shock. On February 21st he was diagnosed, and by April 13th he was dead. Grief had not even had a chance to express itself. However, I found myself living with someone I was afraid of and could not trust. I was deluding myself. I had not even begun to face the unfinished business of agonizing grief. It just loomed over me. And out of fear of not being able to care for my children or myself, I reconciled with my second husband. I was fearful of more abuse, not to mention my doubts of his ever staying away from drugs.

Meanwhile, I was trying to manage my children's grief. My eldest was suffering with depression. My youngest was hanging out with the wrong people, getting too serious over boys. Just barely thirteen years old, she needed her father more than ever. I suffered long over my children, wanting so much for their world to make sense again. So out of desperation, I convinced myself, that at least this man was better than no man at all.

Unstable, yes, I was completely unstable. From June through the end of August, the charade seemed to be working. Then Mark, who was also bipolar, became manic. And with his mania came drug-seeking behaviors—to the emergency room with a broken toe for narcotics; the non-existing migraines for more narcotics. All that led back to crack cocaine and bizarre behaviors. Of course, he lied to cover up. I scrambled to catch him in a lie, but he always blamed me. He seemed so convincing, leaving me feeling like the insane one. When the depression came, he needed heroin to come off the crack cocaine.

Needless to say, our marriage was over. After being escorted out of my home by police, he became desperate. He broke into our doctor's office because he had no money to score drugs. Then he stole checks from his family and held up a grocery store. He left craziness and confusion in his wake. "Drug addicts and alcoholics are like tornados running through the lives of others." (Alcoholics Anonymous)

In addition, I had a hurricane inside me from the bottled up grief and pain. I had lost John, the one person who was always there for me. I had lost the connection of a fifteen-year marriage without closure. I still felt guilty for having walked away from him and my children. The marriage was broken, but we both were broken. The question was, "Did I love this other man too?" Yes, he was a reflection of my broken, wounded self. Maybe, I thought, if I could save him, I could save myself. Or perhaps, because I hated myself and knew I caused others pain, maybe this was all I deserved.

Then, yet another blow came when two detectives stood at my front door. I thought they had come to tell me that Mark had been arrested. Instead, they had found him dead from an overdose of heroin. Just seven months since my first husband had died, I laid my second husband to rest. Both men were dead at the age of 46. I felt numb. It was as if I were having a bad dream. If only I could wake up. This was long-suffering.
I began to question, "God hasn't my life been bad enough? Is this punishment for *every* sin I've committed? How can a loving God

permit such horrible things to happen? Wasn't the abuse of my childhood enough—incest, neglect, abandonment, physical and verbal abuse? Why couldn't this loving God cut me a little slack now? Anger set in, one of the many stages of grief. What should I be angry at—Abuse, Divorce, Cancer, Addictions or Death? No, it had to be someone, not something. Should I be angry at my father, my mother, my counselor, my pastor and all the others for not being there to help me through the most difficult times of my adult life? Yes, all of the above—and God, the one most responsible. Where was He though all of it anyway?

I was full of self-pity and sorrow (sorrow too massive to articulate). I had a sense of hopelessness, like a hole swallowing me up. I wanted to die, not by suicide, just die. If only death would take me so I wouldn't hurt anymore. I could no longer tolerate my own pain, let alone the pain I saw in my children's faces—the kind of pain a mother hopes to protect her children from. It seemed I had no control over my life.

Life continued to hurl its punches. Blow number three came when my son was diagnosed with life-debilitating scoliosis. Surgery was the only hope to keep his organs from crowding as he matured. But he had no health insurance. Silently I screamed, "God, where are you?" No answer. I knew it was *my* responsibility to come up with a solution. Unfortunately, my mind wasn't capable of thinking rational thoughts.

Just when I thought hell had thrown all but the kitchen sink at me, my son said, "Mom, I need help." "What kind of help?" When he didn't respond, I impatiently asked again, "What kind of help?" If I thought things couldn't possibly get any worse, I was sadly mistaken! Finally he answered, "Mom, I hear voices!" My ears began to ring. Silently, I cried out, "Oh, God, he's not just depressed; my son is mentally ill."

The two men I had loved, right or wrong, were now gone. With time I would be able to accept this and move on. But, now my son—just sixteen and a half—my own flesh and blood, had been diagnosed with Schizoaffective Disorder—a combination of bipolar and schizophrenia.

In most cases, trauma is the onset. The first symptom of deep depression appeared when his dad and I divorced. Once a straight-A student, he began failing. Then at the age of 15, he was diagnosed as learning disabled. Symptoms of the disease included voices in his head that interfered with his capacity to concentrate. Thus, the learning disability. Certainly his father's death and the apparent suicide of his step-father were traumatic enough for anyone, let alone him. It was only by the grace of God that I didn't lose *my* mind. However, remembering the sovereignty of God, His hand was upon me, even when I was angry with Him.

Though I didn't know it at the time, God was about to show himself to me. My son's illness was now being managed with psychotropic drugs. Now it was time to address his scoliosis. My best friend told me about the Shriners. I contacted them and they took his case. After many trips to the Shriners Children's Hospital in Philadelphia, they scheduled his surgery in November of 2003.

During the months before his surgery, I stayed depressed and suffered with chronic pain from a compressed disc in my neck. I was put on strong pain medication, which intensified the depression. For the next six months I stayed in bed. I remember, so vividly, looking in the mirror and seeing that I had not showered in probably seven days. I wondered, "Who is this woman, with vacant eyes?" This was the same woman who finally told God she'd had enough. I refused to read my Bible, go to church, and pray. Why pray to a God who seems absent and uncaring? A God who would bring my life down in every way imaginable? Not I! I had had enough!

So I vegetated for almost six months. I could not cope with life. No hope. No energy. No will to even exist. The only reason I lived was because my children needed me. To make matters worse, I mismanaged money so I could not pay all my bills. All our medical expenses came out of pocket. With no insurance, prescription drugs easily ran from $500-$600 per month. Now as the surgery date drew near, I began to have panic attacks. The solution was more drugs—valium. Thank God, I was not drinking, too. On some level the medication made me numb. But, knowing about substance abuse, I realized this couldn't be good. The feelings and emotions simply waited for me. The day of reckoning would come.

Leaving my comfort zone to head to Philadelphia caused paralyzing fear. But I had to put on a mask for the world. Acting as if I had everything under control was probably my best performance yet. Even when I wasn't communicating with God, He was watching me, along with the angels sent to protect and guide me. *"For He will give His angels charge concerning you, to guard you in all ways"* (Psalm 91:11). I'm certain on many occasions they have saved my life. For in the past, I had endangered myself and others.

On my forty-second birthday, my son went into surgery at 7:30 a.m. for major spinal repair. Surgeons placed metal rods in his back to straighten a 70-degree curve in his spine. Twelve long hours we waited. My mom, my step-dad, my daughter, my closest friend, and my oldest sister tried to celebrate my birthday. However, the greatest gift that day was having them there to support us. Most importantly, God had found a way to meet a huge need in my son's life. Once again, God was ever present. However, in my circumstances, I could not, or would not, see it.

My son was wheeled out of surgery at 7:30 that evening. He was pumped so full of fluids that his eyes were almost swollen shut. And he was on a respirator, unable to breathe on his own. Such a frightening sight for any parent! He tried to call out to me, but it was all garbled. As they wheeled him into the recovery room, I tried to compose myself, saying my goodbyes to everyone. Now that everyone had left, I went back to the intensive care unit to sit with my son. However, he continued to try to talk to me. So the ICU nurse made it clear that I would have to leave.

Upset and lonely, I walked to the roof of the building where I could smoke. At that time, cigarettes were my "life savers." After that, I went to the room provided for me. What a blessing! The Shriners organized everything. As I walked into my hotel room, I reached for the remote control to the TV. For the past six months I had used TV to escape my internal pain. I don't believe that in the year and a half since my first husband's death and the year since my second husband's death I ever really allowed myself to grieve. Between their deaths and my son's illness I became afraid to feel. If I gave in to the emotion, I thought I would never come up out of the intensity of my despair. It would be the death of me.

When the TV came on, a woman said, "I love Jesus!" I thought, "Oh, great, just what I need!" Believe me, It was meant with all sarcasm. When I looked, I saw a woman with pink hair—Jan Crouch of Trinity Broadcasting Network. Today I know it was a divine appointment. But, when she said, "I love Jesus!" it brought more rage then I knew I was capable of. I tried to sort through the clothes in my suitcases. It is funny now. I was so overwhelmed and depressed that I packed enough luggage to go on a cruise. I couldn't put two thoughts together. Making decisions was next to impossible. Now at that moment, all I wanted was something to sleep in. I screamed at God, as I pulled out every piece of clothing, throwing it around the room. I snapped. I don't think God was surprised at my behavior. However, it did surprise me. God Himself had set me up, even with all my unbridled anger and hatred.

I felt a Presence filling the room. I had an encounter with God, Himself. He made sure I had no other place to go. I remember screaming at Him saying, "Why? What did I do to deserve this much pain? I can't do this! I can't do this! It's me, Terrie, the weak one! The alcoholic! This is too much for me!" The anger changed to a sob that came from the core of my being. Falling to my knees, I said in between desperate sobs, "I'm sorry! I'm so sorry!" The Presence became so strong. If I could have seen into the spirit realm, the Lord Himself would have been visible in my little hotel room. He spoke to me, not with an audible voice, but a voice that quieted, and interrupted my thoughts.

"Terrie, I never asked you to do any of it. I just wanted you to look at me. Don't turn to the right. Don't turn to the left. Just look to me, for I am the glory and the lifter of your head" (Psalm 3:3). There is a time under the sun for everything. There is an appointed time for everything... *"a time to weep and a time to laugh; a time to mourn and a time for dance"* (Ecclesiastes 3:4). You have honored and mourned both your husbands. Now, I'm going to pour so much joy on you that you will not be able to contain it."

I was still weeping uncontrollably in His Presence. Almost two years of grief and pain continued to pour out of me. The anointing was strong in the room that night. I may have been crying tears of pain so far back I wouldn't remember. His Word says the anointing heals yokes and bondages in our lives. I spoke again, "Tell me what to do. I'll do anything; just tell me what to do."

Very clearly, He said, "I want you to forgive." As He said this, names came to my mind, "your father, your mother, your counselor, and your pastor Jerry."

At that point, I spoke, "But God, they abandoned me."

He said, "No, Terrie, they didn't abandon you. I'm a sovereign God. I didn't let them come. I wanted you all to myself."

The King of Kings, the Lord of Lords, wanted me all to Himself. This God, who I had thought abandoned me, wanted me. This was a love that had suffered long. He had suffered long *for* me and *with* me. I continued to forgive as He had asked. Then I had a flash-back. My life unfolded before my eyes, a messed up and crazy life. Once again, the Lord responded to my thoughts.
He said, "I have a call on your life."

Immediately, I had a vision. I never had a vision before, or one since. I was standing on a platform speaking to a lot of people, mostly women. All of a sudden, I knew none of my experiences had been in vain. He could use my broken pieces to bring people to salvation and the healing power of the Lord, Jesus Christ.

He said, "I will pick up the broken pieces, and use all the fragments of your life."

Now I understood. *"We love because He first loved us"* (1 John 4:19). God saved my life that night, not eternally, for I already was His. Instead He saved me from the deadness of my life. The process began that night and will continue until I see Him face to face.

"Being confident of this, that he who began a good work in you will carry it on to completion" (Philippians 1:6). *"For He is the Author and Perfecter of our faith"* (Hebrews 12:2). He came to set the captives free, and to give us life more abundantly. What a loving Father. Yes, like none I'd ever known!

Long-suffering, what does it really mean? It means perseverance, patience, and self-control even when it hurts. It was depicted first and in total perfection by our Savior and Lord, Jesus Christ. For our sins, the Messiah suffered crucifixion, the most despised and shameful death. It was a criminal's death for a sinless man. He bore the cross to die in our place as a ransom for us all. He hung and bled for our sins so we could have a relationship with a perfect God. Since He sees us through the eyes of grace, He suffered long so we could have His righteousness. As He was being nailed to the cross, our sins were too, once and for all.

Our part is to believe in our hearts and confess with our mouths that Jesus Christ is Lord (Romans 10:9-10). We need to acknowledge that He died so that we could live. From His example, we learn to bear our cross daily. We are to suffer long, accepting His will over ours. We can know His will by having a relationship with Him. We must listen to His still, small voice which guides us. *"My sheep hear my voice, and I know them, and they follow me"* (John 10:27).

In my life, suffering came through the things I had experienced, things I could not control and the things I was responsible for. I was learning to persevere—running the race to win. At times I was forgiving, not because I felt like it, but because He demands it. *"But if you do not forgive others, then your Father will not forgive your transgressions"* (Matthew 6:15). I am to bless others when persecuted, spoken badly of, and hurt through their behaviors. I am to love others with the patience and mercy God extends to me.

"Brethren, I do not regard myself as having laid hold of it yet; but one thing I do: forgetting what lies behind and reaching forward to what lies ahead" (Philippians 3:13). Press on to the upward call of God in Christ Jesus. Do everything as unto the Lord. Long-suffering and perseverance bring godly character. It is never easy, but is always worth it. We are tested as with fire, purifying us as like gold. Long-suffering is part of the sanctification process.

Out of desperation, I cried out to the Lord in the hotel room that night. *"Whoever calls upon the name of the Lord shall be saved"* (Romans 10:13). The Word is truth; that night that scripture took on new meaning. He not only gives us salvation, but He also saves us from our fears, our weaknesses, and all our shame. *"The sacrifices of God are a broken spirit; a broken and a contrite heart, O God, You will not despise"* (Psalm 51:17).

God knows when our heart is fully His. And in that moment, He filled me with His power to become the over-comer He created me to be. We are victorious in Him. In our weakness the Lord is made strong. *"Consider Him who endured such hostility by sinners against Himself, so that we would not grow weary and lose heart"* (Hebrews 12:3). No, it may not be easy, but I am to follow Christ's example. I am to endure. But if I remember what He did for me, suddenly, I become willing to press in harder, knowing that *"I can do all things through Christ who strengthens me"* (Philippians 4:13).

I continued to endure and suffer through many things. One heart-breaking incident was that my son became paranoid of me. Paranoia of caregivers is common to his illness. Of all things, he latched onto my unwavering faith in God. He said I claimed to be a prophet; he believed I was living in deception. Therefore, he had to escape my care. He left me to live with his father's family. I lost my son because of his delusions. I had to let him go and trust God to watch over him while he was away from me.

Three years later, my daughter, married at the age of 19. I felt she was giving up on all the dreams I had for her. Feeling totally abandoned, now by my daughter, I had to find a way not to feel all alone. There is no perfection in this human body. And His Word clearly warns, *"Therefore let him who thinks he stands take heed that he does not fall"* (1 Corinthians10:12). *"And blessed is he who does not take offense at Me"* (Matthew 11:6). I had taken an offense and did not realize it.

Once more I opened myself up to the lies of the enemy. He said, "You are alone again, and always will be." I had not totally allowed the Lord to heal the scars of abandonment. My unresolved feeling had waited for me. So even after all I'd learned, all I had experienced with the Lord, I once again fell from grace. I drank so hard that I put everything that meant the world to me in jeopardy: my children, my ministry, my job, and all the blessings God had given to me. If I had continued the way I was going, death was inevitable.

"When the unclean spirit goes out of a man, it passes through waterless places seeking rest, and not finding any, it says, I will return to my house from which I came. And when it comes, it finds it swept and put in order. Then it goes and takes along seven other spirits more evil than itself, and they go in and live there; and the last state of that man becomes worse than the first" (Luke11:24-26). As for me, it seemed he brought a *lot* more than seven.

Believe me, I have experienced the truth of his Word regarding this. However, God, in His faithfulness, His infinite mercy—mercy that is new every morning—suffered long once again. Just as the father ran to meet the prodigal son, so my loving Father pulled me from the pit again. When I blatantly disgraced His name—the name I had always been open in sharing with everyone—He still rescued me. I was always so grateful for His love and everything He had done for me. Although He did not make it easy, He provided a way of escape. Once again, in my weakness, He showed Himself strong. And just like with the prodigal, He didn't just feed me bread and water, or punish me for my sin. As I repented once again, He was faithful and just to forgive and cleanse me from all unrighteousness. (1 John 1:9).

Through that experience, I learned yet a deeper level of His love. I fell more in love with Him. My obedience comes from my love for Him. I have found there is suffering, whether by our own hands, for the cause of Christ, or because of life's painful circumstances that may be orchestrated by the devil. However, God knows what we need in our lives, and because of His sovereignty, He allows us to suffer at times. Things are meant for our growth. His Word says, *"Consider it all joy, my brethren, when you encounter various trials, knowing that the testing of your faith produces endurance"* (James 1:2-3). Those that endure to the end shall be saved (Matthew 10:22).

I see long-suffering as three kinds. First, the kind our Lord showed us at the cross. Second, the kind we will work on until we meet Jesus face-to-face. The suffering God allows in our lives is always for our good—the growing in the wilderness—both before and after salvation. He used the wounds of my past to draw me in desperation, so I would know Him, not just as Savior, but as my Lord. Then last, through the testing of our faith. He may use us as His disciples, *"That you may stand perfect and fully assured in all the will of God"* (Colossians 4:12). Choosing His will first for our lives is Christ's ultimate goal for the believer.

Long-suffering will always be a part of the mature Christian's life, but what does change is our willingness to go through. Through each and every experience, we learn to trust in Him more. *"All things work together for good to those that love the Lord, and are called according to His purpose"* (Romans 8:28). It is all about Him. We are to love Him with all our strength, with our soul, and with all our heart, so that we may be used of Him, that by His love, His fruit may be seen in us.

As Paul stated, *"But whatever things were gain to me, those things I counted as loss for the sake of Christ. More than that, I count all things to be as loss in view of the surpassing value of knowing Christ Jesus my Lord, for whom I have suffered the loss of all things, and count them but rubbish so that I may gain Christ, and may be found in Him not having a righteousness of my own derived from the law, but that which is through faith in Christ, the righteousness which comes from God on the basis of faith, that I may know Him and the power of His resurrection and the fellowship of his sufferings, being conformed to His death; in order that I may attain to the resurrection from the dead. Not that I have already obtained it or have already become perfect, but I press on so that I may lay hold of that for which I also was laid hold of by Christ Jesus"* (Philippians 3:7-14).

"For the Spirit of the Lord is upon me, because The Lord has anointed me, to bring good news to the afflicted; He has sent me to bind up the broken hearted, to proclaim liberty to the captives, And freedom to the prisoners, To proclaim the favorable year of our Lord . . ." (Isaiah 61:1-3).

"By their fruit you will know them, so that they may see our good works, that our Father in Heaven may be glorified" (Matthew 5:16).

Serenity Prayer

*God, grant me the serenity
to accept the things I cannot change,
the courage to change the things I can,
and the wisdom to know the difference.
Living one day at a time,
enjoying one moment at a time;
accepting hardship as a pathway to peace;
taking, as Jesus did, this sinful world as it is;
not as I would have it;
trusting that You will make all things right
if I surrender to Your will;
so that I may be reasonably happy in this life
and supremely happy with You
forever in the next.
Amen
-Reinhold Niebuhr*

Terrie Bryan

Kindness, Gentleness and Goodness

"Therefore, as God's chosen people,
holy and dearly loved,
clothe yourselves with compassion,
kindness, humility, gentleness and
patience. Bear with each other and
forgive whatever grievances you
may have against one another.
Forgive as the Lord forgave you."

Colossians 3:12-13

It has taken me quite some time in my walk with the Lord to really understand that I am a chosen person, I am God's beloved, and I am dearly loved by the Lord. All my life I doubted if my family really loved me. At times it was scary, frightening, lonely and confusing when growing up in my family. So when I was told about Jesus dying for me—and that He loved me—well, that was unbelievable to me.

When I accepted Christ as my personal Savior, I began to change. You see, I was the one described as the little teapot ready to boil and spout off at anytime. I struggled with anger and a not-so-nice temper. I had hurts and fears that I was unable to express. So I expressed them by blowing up. I suppressed all those doubts and fears until they slowly came to that boil. And you know what happens when the teapot is boiling—it whistles and spews everywhere.

Jesus slowly began to do a work in me. But first He had to start healing the wounds that I had. Those wounds were the pains of my parents' divorce, their remarriages, step-parents, sexual abuse, fear, uncertainty, insecurities, my looks, and loneliness. As you can see, the devil used all of these things to convince me that God didn't love me. I thought, "If my family can't love me, how can He?"

I didn't want to be that person who blew up all the time; I didn't want to be so defeated. More than anything I wanted to express how I felt without anger ruling my life. I found that the first step is stated so clearly in the scripture: "Forgive whatever grievances you may have against one another. Forgive as the Lord forgave you."

I had to forgive those who had hurt me. Was that going to be easy? I'm sure you can answer that question. No, it was going to be very difficult. At times I had to relive the things I had gone through so I could receive healing. The Bible says, *"So, if the Son sets you free, you will be free indeed"* (John 8:3).

If you struggle, be encouraged that if the Son (Jesus Christ) sets you free, you will be free indeed. He so wants to restore you that you may experience Him fully. When you have come to know Him as your personal Savior, all things old shall pass away and all things are made new. He will begin a work in you so that you can be that clay in the potter's hands. He will begin to mold and shape you into the image of Christ. In return, you will produce the fruit of the Spirit. The Bible says, *"But the fruit of the Spirit is love, joy, peace, patience, kindness, goodness, faithfulness, gentleness and self control. Against such things there is no law"* (Galatians 5:22-23).

It's funny that the women in this book see me as exemplifying the fruit of gentleness and kindness because I don't always see myself that way. Let's look for just a moment at the definition of *kindness*. "Kindness is an eagerness to put others at ease. It is a sweet and attractive temperament that shows friendly regard." Can't you just picture a ripened peach—one that has just been picked off the tree, oozing with sweetness, and tender to eat.

Before knowing Christ I saw myself as an angry and harsh person. Now knowing Christ, I can be merciful, sweet and tender. It is only the Lord who can do that kind of work in a person's life *"But when the kindness and love of God our Savior appeared, He saved us, not because of righteous things we had done, but because of His mercy. He saved us through the washing of rebirth and renewal by the Holy Spirit"* (Titus 3:4-5).

I can only give praise to the Lord for what He has done in my life. Growing up, no one ever put me at ease, telling me that God was in control. No one said that everything was going to be all right because we serve a big God. Because that was never conveyed to me, instability ruled my life. I came to a place in my walk with the Lord where I needed to place my trust in Him, not man.

The Lord became my constant, my strength and my security. I took my sight off the adults in my life and placed my life into the Lord's hands because He alone is faithful. *"The LORD Himself goes before you and will be with you; He will never leave you nor forsake you"* (Deuteronomy 31:8). I don't know about you, but it makes me want to shout to the roof tops of what my God can do for me. The kindness and the love that Christ showed us by giving His life for us is the same kindness that we must show to others.

Let's take a look at another fruit of the Spirit, *Gentleness*. The definition of gentleness is "a humble, non-threatening demeanor that comes from a position of strength and authority and is useful in calming another's anger." Gentleness is not a quality that is weak and passive. I laughed a little when looking at this fruit definition— "useful in calming another's anger." See what the Lord can do, He took me from being angry and enabled me through the Spirit to calm another's anger. Gentleness is not a dictator, lording over people. It is helping them to reach fullness in their walk with the Lord. It's a calming to individuals who may be restless in their walk. Gentleness is giving people that slight nudge to move forward.

So often in these days and times there are a lot of demands from full time jobs, children, husbands, and meetings. Then we get under pressure and suppress the fruit of gentleness. That is where Satan wants us to be—so bogged down that we become uptight and tired. Then we become snappy and irritable. That's when we have to arise, push through the tough times, and exemplify the fruit of the Spirit. Jesus said, *"Come to me, all who are weary and burdened, and I will give you rest. Take my yoke upon you and learn from me, for I am gentle and humble in heart, and you will find rest for your souls. For my yoke is easy and my burden is light"* (Matthew 21:5). Jesus has been there for me when I have become weary and burdened with daily life. In the times when the battle has been its toughest, I can look back and see that He gave the rest and strength I needed. And He will give you the same rest. However, we have to rely upon Him. Looking back, I often tried to do it on my own. But, as we've seen from His Word, He wants us to rely upon Him.

We could define the fruit of the Spirit *Goodness* as "one who is generous to give to others what is not deserved , an encourager to others." I love to see others built up, rather than torn down. I'm one who enjoys lifting others up in their walk.

When it came to encouragement, my family members were wreckers. They were suspicious people, bitter about another's blessings, and never excited for others' endeavors. Instead of looking for the good in people, they sought the negatives. I remember when I was fourteen, sharing with my aunt, "I'd love to go away to college one day and be a business woman. Maybe even owning my own business. She looked at me and said, "Yeah right! You will never amount to anything like that!" I was so hurt and so discouraged. I thought, "She's probably right! I will never be able to do that."

The enemy wanted me to feel defeated. But I persevered and later went to college for a couple of years. And I had the experience of working in the business world. Now the Lord has given me the opportunity to serve on staff at my church. I oversee all of the other staff members. When trusting and resting in the Lord, He will give you the desires of your heart. His word shows us: *"Delight yourself in the LORD and He will give you the desires of your heart"* (Psalm 37:4).

My dad's brothers and sisters would get angry and fight as adults because they thought someone was talking about them. They called the extended family members "trash" seeking to tear them down. But the Lord began to show me His goodness—He was generous to give to me what I did not deserve. I didn't deserve His forgiveness and mercy, but He gave it to me. He gave me victory; He gave me love; He was gentle. He spoke so sweetly and softly to me, telling me He loved me, and He wanted to be a part of my life. He wanted to be the father that I didn't have at that time.

Once in a church service the Pastor said, "Do you feel like you have no one? Do you have a real father who isn't a part of your life? I began to cry because that was me. I didn't feel like I had anyone because at that time I hadn't spoken to my dad in months. I wanted him to be in my life; I wanted him to be concerned about what I was doing; and I so wanted him to love me. My dad was not able to share in conversation about what was going on in *my* life. He was more concerned about what was happening in *his*.

The devil is out to tear down what the Lord wants to do in your life. He wants you to believe that you have no one, you are alone, and no one cares about you. The devil doesn't want you to live the abundant life because He wants to invoke the negatives and his lies upon your life.

I was looking at the Pastor thinking, "Yes, that's me." He said, "Jesus is there for you. He loves you, and He wants to be your Father. He wants to fill those voids that you are feeling right now. Come to the altar, and He will meet you there." That Sunday morning Jesus did meet me there, and I came to know Him as my personal Savior.

"Surely goodness and mercy will follow me all the days of my life, and I will dwell in the house of the LORD forever" (Psalm 23:6).

The Bible says that you will dwell in the house of the Lord forever. How exciting is that! That's goodness to me—He gave me life even when I didn't deserve it.

In all of this, how do we rely upon Jesus and live an abundant life? We must come to Him:

Through His Word
Through our prayer
Always watching and waiting
Prepared to act on His expressed desires
Ready to give an account
With a trained heart responsive to His voice
Confessing our sins and wrong doings
Through praise and worship

The list above has been crucial to my walk with the Lord. I encourage you to seek after the heart of God—to rest in Him. Then you will be exhibiting the fruit of kindness, gentleness and goodness in your walk with Christ. The world offers a lot of coldness and emptiness in the hearts and lives of both young and old. We can be that beacon of hope to individuals by offering to them mercy, tenderness, calmness, and encouragement through the fruit of gentleness, kindness and goodness.

Prayer:

Dear Heavenly Father,

I thank you for giving your son Jesus so that I may have life. Thank you that even when I was undeserving of your forgiveness that you were generous to me. I ask that you will heal the wounds that I may carry from the hurts of the past. I ask Jesus that you will restore me. I ask that you will make me whole. Holy Spirit I ask that you will help me to exhibit the fruit of kindness, gentleness and goodness. Help me in my walk that I will put you first and that I will seek you with my whole heart. Thank you for what you're going to do in and through me. Thank you for the victory that I have in you Jesus.

In Jesus Name Amen.

Paula Conner

JOY

*"You have made known to me the
path of life;
You will fill me with Joy in Your
presence."*

Psalms 16:11

There was no joy in my life for years. For 36 years, from age 12 to 48, I looked *down* to where I was—not *up* to where I could be. I didn't believe, or even wonder, if my life could change. But today I'm a living, breathing testimony to God's mercy and long-suffering. Believe me, when I tell you, "Where there is life, there is hope!"

How did I go wrong? Raised in church, a "good girl" in an ordinary family, I was trained up in the way I should go. Yet for years I disobeyed God. I actually knew better, but I was running, hiding, scheming and working my plans. I disregarded God and didn't consider Him in any part of my life.

It's scary to think how many of us "Baby Boomers" slipped from our parents and family into a world gone crazy. The 1950's and 1960's brought TV, Elvis, Rock and Roll, the Beatles, the Vietnam War, and drugs. Everywhere you heard, "You deserve a break today!" "Make love, not war!" "You've come a long way, Baby!" "Women's Lib!" and "If it feels good, do it!"

Like the people of old, we laughed at the prophets of doom and gloom. We were a godly nation who enjoyed the blessings of post-war jubilation and success. The "woe to you" message fell on deaf ears. The ruler of the air swept into every living room. Music, advertising, coarse humor, propaganda and lessons on "how to do" the wrong things filled our eyes and ears; they headed straight for our hearts.

Our minds were being changed for the worse. It was a slow process like boiling a frog alive: First, put the frog in a pot of cold water where he will happily swim around. Next, add a little heat. To him it's a nice, warm bath. Gradually turn up the heat. Without his ever realizing it, he's been boiled alive—done. That's where we were— little by little—on the way to being "done."

Our parents never had a chance, but they didn't know it. They thought if they disciplined us, we would straighten up and change our ways. Not so! Instead, a whole generation of children chose selfishness—handed to us on a silver platter. None of us knew the price we would have to pay.

I was a "goody-goody" at home, acting the way my parents want- ed. But outside in the world, I was an actress in the making, and a pretty good one at that. Learning to walk both sides of the fence, I became a deceiver, a sinner, and a man-pleaser.

I had no idea what Satan had planned for me. But gradually, day by day, I sank deeper and deeper into a dark "pit of despair." Satan left not one stone unturned. There was no way out on my own. My sin had put a lid on my conscience. And shame kept me from seeking the light.

But "God will make a way where there seems to be no way." Like the Israelites in the wilderness, I was just inches away from the Promised Land. Yet I kept making wrong turns away from Him. I thought there was no hope for me. But, God!

When I was 28 years old, God gave me a glimpse of eternity and His grace. Finally I understood the meaning of Jesus' blood sacri- fice and what it meant for me. I was in awe of God, and for a few years I respected the line drawn in the sand for me. I listened to tel- evangelists and read my Bible, as well as other Christian books.

But even during that time my mind was not transformed. James 1:22 says it best. I was a *hearer* of the word only, not a *doer*—a person who looks at herself and sees good. Then she goes away and does evil, still a deceiver, a sinner, and a man-pleaser.

After a couple of serious, obvious slips, I was back on the road to Hell. Satan told me I was a hypocrite, so I quit trying. I took a turn for the worse. My course was set – "Down Hill from Here" was my sign!

My testimony is like the prodigal son's. By the grace of God, one day I came to myself. Then I remembered the relief, the peace and the joy I had back when God (in His perfect timing) had shown up. All I said was, "God, if you will take me back to that moment, I will serve you wholeheartedly." And He did! Can you believe it? He did! He could see my *heart*—a heart that was really seeking Him.

My Lord filled me with power and strength to resist the old temptations. Best of all, He changed my life for good, just as He promised. My main support during the last 12 years has been the Word of God. Our local gospel radio station and my church, Tree of Life Ministries, have provided nourishment to feed my spirit.

As a parent, you wouldn't think of leaving your child for days neglected and unfed. Likewise, the Spirit who lives in you will fade away if not fed. Ignoring the Word of God opens the door for Satan to come in. So diligently feed your Spirit the Word of God, and His fruit will be your reward.

All the fruit of the Spirit have been evident on my journey. However, *Joy* was the last to show up. My human nature was critical and bossy. People walked around me to keep from getting stuck. I still have a long way to go. But spending time praying, asking, knocking, and seeking have helped to sand off some of the rough edges of my "prickly" personality.

Self confidence, relief from the stress of my sin, and wise choices led to security. These are changes that have come to me supernaturally, because I decided to follow Jesus. God has given me a little confidence prayer. It gives Him glory and gives me courage to do His will: "Father, you have given me the desire to obey you, and I know you will give me the power to please you."

"Every good and perfect gift is from above..." (James 1:17). The desire to obey Him is a gift. If you have the desire to obey, *just do it!* Obedience leads to blessing, and blessing leads to *Joy.* Joy is a powerful force. It inspires us to continue in our obedience. In turn, this pleases God.

Now I can smile without trying. My days flow with purpose, expectation, and completion instead of anxiety, confusion and dread. God has provided for my every need because He knows my heart is to obey Him.

My joy level is always high, not because of a wonderful lifestyle or confidence in myself. But it's because I have the Holy Spirit living in me. His joy in me comes out. When He shows up, I am so overcome that it's hard to hide. Joy is not something you can learn to do. It's not a positive attitude or trying to make yourself happy with things. The first step is to seek first the kingdom of God. Joy is a gift from God that He supernaturally gives to you when your desire is all for Him. Joy is a feeling you get when you have obeyed God. God's own joy in you is released when you do things the right way. There is no better feeling than being in the will of God through obedience to His Word.

Joy is like a magnet that draws others to you. Scripture tells us, *"...the joy of the Lord is your strength"* (Nehemiah 8:10). Think about it. The joy and the strength you have is the Lord's, not yours. You are the vessel, a container for God's joy.

Without His Spirit living in you, you can be happy for a while. You can be debt-free, have a fine home and car; get a great education and secure job; give birth to beautiful and healthy children; try your best to raise them in a normal home; and have all the outward signs of success. But if the Lord doesn't build the house, you are wasting your time (Psalm 127:1). If the Spirit is not at work in your life, there is no joy.

The fruit of God's own Spirit has to come from Him. You are powerless to produce it on your own. Your strength to fight Satan and be delivered from his worldly snares comes from the joy of the Lord.

There is a train that runs through our minds all the time. A steady stream of words never stops rolling. Sometimes the words are hopeful, uplifting and healthy. At other times, we get off on another track where the words roll out guilt, shame, discouragement, envy, jealousy, self pity or fear. That train is on the way to death and the pit.

When the Holy Spirit of God comes to dwell in us, He comforts and steers us back onto the right track. All the time He is showing us what is true and what is false. Overtime, my life has become a source of joy for me. The things I used to say to myself—words of self-pity and shame—have stopped getting through.

Our thoughts are seeds, producing more of the same. My plan of attack—to change my thoughts—had to be a cold-turkey approach. It took a while to realize what was happening. But then I knew what I had to do. I stopped listening to any music, TV or radio shows that helped fill the "train to the pit." I didn't have to worry. The Holy Spirit helped me through this. Also, I began a devotional/journal that inspired thoughts and prepared fertile soil to receive from God. As unworthy as I was, I started looking for other women who loved God. I wanted to change the destination of my train. So I got serious about finding the purpose for my life. God's will then became the focus of my search. I walked away from the old temptations that shamed me into isolation—a dark place with no hope.

You have to call Satan out, expose him, and tell him that you see him for who he is. Rebuke him in Jesus' name. He has to flee! Then God gives you the strength to turn from your wicked ways so He can heal you.

Walking away left me with a clean, clear conscience and into a place where Satan was out of bounds. I was free! God's light began to shine on me—a warm, soft, smiling light made me feel loved. In His presence there is joy, freedom, life and hope. There is no other way to be whole.

Are you empty? Are you weak, sick and tired? Are you broken or abused? Are you searching for an answer to a question you can't even put into words? Jesus is the answer. Would you like some peace? Are you worried or helpless? Are you looking for a God worthy of your worship? Has Satan convinced you there is no hope for you—that it's over, and no one can help you? Remember, Satan is a liar. Jesus Christ has died so all of your questions could be answered. I pray for you today, that the desire to have your questions answered becomes so strong that you will close your eyes and call out the name of "Jesus." He is your only hope.

Each one of us has to come to the place where we "grow-up." We must stop whining over our lives—offending others and being offended. God has a plan for each of us. He knows best, even if we still play the world's game, remaining in our selfish little shell, moaning, "What about me?"

God expectantly waits for us like the father in Luke 15. He jumps up and down with joy when we finally lay down our "baby selves" and turn to Him for joy and purpose in our lives.

Be encouraged and comforted as you confess the Word of God regarding the God of *Joy*.

"Have mercy on me, O Lord, for I call to you all day long. Bring joy to your servant, for to you, O Lord, I lift up my soul. You are forgiving and good, O Lord, abounding in love to all who call to you" (Ps. 86: 3-5).

"I will be glad and rejoice in your love, for you saw my affliction and knew the anguish of my soul" (Ps. 31:7).

"Let me hear joy and gladness; let the bones you have crushed rejoice. Restore to me the joy of your salvation and grant me a willing spirit, to sustain me" (Ps. 51:8, 12).

"For His anger lasts only a moment, but His favor lasts a lifetime; weeping may remain for a night, but rejoicing comes in the morning. . . You turned my wailing into dancing; you removed my sackcloth and clothed me with joy" (Ps. 30:5, 11).

Prayer:

Dear Heavenly Father, thank you for the revelation of your joy. I pray that I will become an instrument in your hand. Use me to demonstrate your joy to others, that you might receive the glory. Amen.

Mary Wagner

SELF-CONTROL

"Thy kingdom come, Thy will be done,
on earth as it is in heaven."

Matthew 6:10

Is self-control outdated? In the world where we live, we see little evidence of it. Increasingly, our present day looks more like the time of the Old Testament judges where everyone did what was right in his own eyes. As we look around us, it seems that self-control has indeed become an outdated virtue. Our world's motto is, "If it feels good do it."

God's Words tells us, *"Now those who belong to Christ have cru-cified the flesh with its passions and desires. If we live by the Spirit, let us also walk by the Spirit"* (Gal. 5:24-25). I believe this passage speaks powerfully about where the fruit of self-control originates.

When a lost and dying world examines the lives of God's people, we don't appear any different from those who are of the world. In fact, sometimes our lives appear more out of control because we try to walk out our faith in our flesh, rather than in the Spirit. The Galatians passage speaks of the crucifixion of the flesh. A death of crucifixion can only happen with the help of someone else. In a lit-eral sense, crucifixion is death on a cross. There is no way that can be accomplished alone. Christ's crucifixion required that He allow someone else to pound the nails into His hands and His feet.

If we desire to have our fleshly passions and desires crucified, there is only One who can help us with the pounding of those nails lead-ing to the death of that flesh. That One is Jesus. In allowing Him to choose those experiences that will cause our flesh to decrease, we are surrendering our will to His. This is just as Jesus did when He went to the cross for us. When we allow our God to crucify our flesh, we will then become increasingly kingdom-of-God minded. I believe this is what John meant in his gospel when he said, *"He must increase, but I must decrease"* (John 3:30). When this is allowed to happen, we become all about advancing His Kingdom rather than the kingdom of self. We will also see the fruit of self-control come forth in our lives.

The Lord taught me an important lesson early on in my walk with Him about surrendering my will to His. Because my walk with Him didn't begin until I was in my middle 30's, I had much of the world's teaching woven into who I was.

The Lord came into my life at a time when I was struggling mightily to recover from the effects of being sexually abused as a young child. I was repeatedly sexually abused by my father's best friend. Because of that, I developed a long list of issues that I dragged around with me. I suffered severe depression and anxiety for most of my life. Moreover, I developed an eating disorder. The result of this was that at a low point in my life I weighed well over 300 pounds.

Fear was woven into the very fabric of who I was. It ruled each and every decision I made. A devastating time came when I had to spend some time in a psychiatric unit. I spent all that I had, from a financial standpoint, looking for healing from all of the issues that this abuse had caused me. It had happened so early in my life that it really shaped who I was. Its effects literally ruled my life from the day I could remember anything.

I spent 12 years in secular counseling offices searching for help. I experienced times when I would improve, but I always returned to a worse place. Even after I came to know the Lord, I still struggled in this way.

One day after I had been saved, I was in a Christian bookstore and found myself standing in front of a collection of books on healing from sexual abuse. Yet again I was at a low point in my quest for healing. I can remember praying, "God, please help me to buy the book that will help me get better and stay that way."

I had read many secular books on this subject, but had not read any Christian works on it. That day the Lord led me to buy a book entitled, "The Wounded Heart". It related what sexual abuse does to the spirit of the sufferer. Never had I read anything that addressed the spiritual aspect of the issue. As I began to read, I saw myself on every page. All I could think was, "Someone finally gets it!" What I never had the words to express or the spirit to understand quickly became clear to me through its pages. The book was tremendously healing for me. But then I got to the last chapter. It was about forgiving your abuser. I slammed the book shut and refused to read it! The Lord allowed me to put the book away for a year. In His mercy, God used that year to prepare me. When the time of preparation was over, He began to speak to me about the issue of forgiveness once more.

About the same time the sermon at the church I was attending was "Praying for Your Enemies." At the end of the sermon, the pastor's instructions were to seek the Lord and ask Him, "Whom shall I pray for?" We were to pray for the person God directed us to for a period of three weeks. I asked the Lord, and He said it was time for me to begin praying for my abuser. And He promised to help me. I was still very reluctant to think about this man, let alone pray for him. I was angry and bitter about what had happened to me and the way my life had gone. To be very honest with you, I wanted my revenge my way. I wanted to be judge, jury and executioner of this man. I wanted to be in God's place in this situation.

But God had said He would help me to pray, so I began. I can tell you, that was a very long three weeks! Each time I prayed I wept—

sometimes tears of anger or bitterness, sometimes tears of pain, sometimes tears of grief over what I had lost. But at the end of this time, God brought me to a state of utter brokenness before Him. Then He spoke to me and changed my life forever. He said, "I didn't hang on the cross for just your sins; I hung there for your abuser's sins as well." At that point I realized just how much the Lord had helped me. I was able to extend forgiveness to this man and ask God to forgive him as well.

It would be a gross understatement to say this was a major turning point in my walk with the Lord and my healing process! I had been held in the bondage of unforgiveness because I had bought into the world's brand of forgiveness. I believed that the one I was being asked to forgive had to deserve it. I also believed the lie that said if I forgave him, I was admitting that what he had done was not wrong. These two beliefs had been woven into the fabric of my flesh and led to my desire to stand in God's place of judging the man who had harmed me.

During the three weeks of praying for my abuser, God crucified my flesh. The forgiveness He required was very different from what I'd been taught by the world. Forgiving the man who had harmed me so deeply meant that I was releasing him to God-- the One who cared more for me than any other. Moreover, that One who was asking me to forgive had been ever so watchful over my life. He had numbered every one of those tears that I had cried and indeed taken note of my pain (Psalm 56:8). Therefore, I had a choice to make. If I followed my flesh, chances were that my mind, heart and spirit would remain in the same wretched condition it had been in for most of my life. If I allowed the Lord to crucify my flesh and began to walk in the footsteps of Jesus, it would leave room for God to handle this situation justly, from His perspective, not mine.

Romans 12:19 told me exactly what I needed to do. *"Never take your own revenge beloved, but leave room for the wrath of God, for it is written, "Vengeance is mine, I will repay, says the Lord"* My part was to surrender, and He would take care of the situation. As I did this, God opened a door to healing in my life that had never been there before. I believe that if I had not allowed the Lord to pound the nails into my flesh through this experience healing that continues even today would never have taken place. Was the process painful? Yes, flesh does not like to die. Was it worth the price asked? Absolutely! Could I have survived anyone else driving the nails that brought my flesh to death? No one but my Jesus could have accomplished it!

I'd like to share just one more aspect of my forgiveness story with you. When the Lord walked me through this process, I knew that I had honestly forgiven my abuser. There was fruit of that in my life. But every once in a while a little doubt would creep in. You know how it is sometimes. The enemy likes to plant those lying thoughts in your mind. I'm so thankful that we serve a God who speaks to His children today! He does this in various ways.

Sometimes He will speak to me through dreams. Recently He did this regarding my abuser. Through it, I believe the Lord wants you to see what the fruit of your obedience can yield. I share this with you to demonstrate that God is a Man of His Word. As you read the account of this dream I pray that you won't see me but our awesome God. May you know that surrender to His will can produce results that are eternal.

Not too long before I was scheduled to teach a group of women about biblical forgiveness the dream came to me. In the dream I was in a place where I had never been before. There my path crossed with the man who had abused me. I remember seeing him. I couldn't understand how he was alive again since he had died of cancer over two years ago. In the dream he was alive, healthy and much younger. Yet everything that had been repulsive to me about him was now gone. I had no feelings of fear or aversion toward him. I remember being confused in the dream because I thought that we were still on earth, and I knew that no one could come back to life once they were dead. This was where the dream ended.

When I awoke the next morning I didn't remember that I'd had a dream. Often when I get ready for the day I spend some time worshipping the Lord by singing to Him. As I was doing this, the Lord brought the dream back to my remembrance. As I began to seek the Lord about what He was trying to tell me through it, He began speaking. "You were right," He said. "It was not possible for you to see this man on earth the way he had appeared in the dream."

My response was, "Yes, Lord, I suspected that, but I still don't understand. How was it possible for our paths to cross and to see him as healed, whole and well, with all of his repulsiveness taken away?" Then the Lord dropped a bombshell. He said, "The only place that you would be able to see him in such a state would be Heaven." Then I said, "Lord, are you saying what I think you're saying? Is it really possible that you have given me a glimpse into the heavenly realm?"

"Don't you remember those three weeks that I asked you to pray for him all those years ago?", asked the Lord. "They brought him to salvation, and you will see him in heaven again the way you saw him in your dream. Your obedience to pray as I asked, moved My hand. He has been saved and is now in heaven."

We never know what the fruit of the surrender of our will to the Father's may be. The last thing I wanted to do was to pray for that man. But what I saw begin to happen in my life was the Lord drawing me into a place of submitting my will to His. As He has helped me do that, I have seen my life yield the fruit of self-control.

Self-control has manifested itself in several ways. The Lord invited me on a weight-loss journey to shed the excess pounds that my years of overeating produced. Food was my drug of choice; eating was what I did to try to take away my emotional pain. I found as God directed my journey, it came with an ease I never dreamed possible. I believe that is partly because the Lord had worked the fruit of self-control in my life. This journey began in June of 2001 and resulted in a 150-pound weight loss that I have maintained for four years. My journey has been far from perfect, but I know that without the surrender of my will to the Lord's, I wouldn't last even one day. The reality is that my willpower is not enough, and will never be enough. It is only as I allow the Lord to bring forth the fruit of self-control in my life that He allows me to succeed.

Another area of my life where I see the evidence of the fruit of self-control is in fasting. Only the Lord would call someone previously afflicted with Obsessive Compulsive Eating Disorder to be a faster! And yet, He has taken me on many fasting journeys, the longest of which was 40 days. Each time He extends the invitation to fast, I see Him work more self-control into my life. While this has never been the reason that I have undertaken a fast, I do see that as I'm obedient to follow Him, even when I would rather not; He meets me there and transforms my self-will. As my flesh recedes, I find that I am more centered on the things of His Kingdom. Again, without the surrender of my will to His, the fruit of self-control that manifests itself would not be possible on these fasting journeys.

There are perilous days ahead of us. The world we live in foreshadows the attitudes that will increase as the last days draw nearer. We would do well as God's people to cultivate the fruit of self-control in our lives. In a self-centered world, the enemy of our souls loves to tempt us. Self-control is something the Lord works in us as part of His package of promised protection for His children.

The apostle Paul speaks powerfully about the difficult times ahead: *"But realize this, that in the last days, difficult times will come. For men will be lovers of self, lovers of money, boastful, arrogant, revilers, disobedient to parents, ungrateful, unholy, unloving, irreconcilable, malicious gossips, without self-control, brutal, haters of good, treacherous, reckless, conceited, lovers of pleasure rather than lovers of God; holding to a form of godliness, although they have denied its power"* (2 Tim 3:1-5).

It sounds like the times we are living in, doesn't it? Self-will against this kind of temptation will not be enough. The days to come will require that we have the fruit of the Spirit of self-control operating in our lives. Only the Lord can work it in us. My encouragement to you is to begin to allow the Lord to work the fruit of self-control into your life. It will strengthen you for the dangerous days we will face. May your prayer be "Thy kingdom come, thy will be done on earth as it is in heaven." And then may you be willing to surrender yourself into the mighty hand of God to see Him work the fruit of self-control in your life!

Prayer:

Precious and Faithful Father,

May the desire of our hearts be to submit our will to Yours. Thank you Lord, that when we are willing to do that we are safely hidden in the center of your will and our lives point those who are watching to Jesus. A sweet aroma of worship is what we long to be to You!

Jennie Sweeney

About the Authors

Patricia is on the Outreach Ministry Team at her church. She loves to read and spend time with her children and grandchildren. One of her favorite places to relax and talk to the Lord is on the beaches of the Outer Banks.

Joyce is the Minister of Outreach at Tree of Life Ministries. She loves encouraging people on their walk with the Lord, ministering to the lost, and speaking at women's groups. Her new passion is writing Christian books. She enjoys time spent with her children and grandchildren.

Ann is the author of ***God's Grace is Sufficient, Ann***. She ministers to women through her church, Stone Croft Ministries, and at other speaking engagements across the country.

Terrie is in furniture sales and also the Interior Decorator where she works. She enjoys spending time with her family, new grand baby and facilitating the Celebrate Recovery Ministry at Tree of Life Ministries.

Jennie is a part of the Biblical Ministries Institute and Ministry Internship Program at Tree of Life Ministries. She is originally from Pennsylvania but now resides in Lynchburg. The desire of her heart is to see spiritual captives set free.

Paula is the Director of Human Resources at Tree of Life Ministries where she oversees the staff and volunteers. She enjoys spending time with her husband and three children. Realizing every day, she has to trust the Lord with every ounce of her life.

Mary has the gift of hospitality which she uses to serve her church family. She enjoys writing and cooking. Her brother calls her their families "social secretary".

Printed in the United States
202430BV00001B/1-315/P